SPIDERS SET I

TRAPDOOR SPIDERS

Tamara L. Britton
ABDO Publishing Company

visit us at
www.abdopublishing.com

Published by ABDO Publishing Company, 8000 West 78th Street, Edina, Minnesota 55439. Copyright © 2011 by Abdo Consulting Group, Inc. International copyrights reserved in all countries. No part of this book may be reproduced in any form without written permission from the publisher. The Checkerboard Library™ is a trademark and logo of ABDO Publishing Company.

Printed in the United States of America, North Mankato, Minnesota.
042010
092010

 PRINTED ON RECYCLED PAPER

Cover Photo: Peter Arnold
Interior Photos: Alamy pp. 11, 17; Corbis p. 7; Getty Images pp. 9, 15, 21;
    Photo Researchers pp. 5, 19; Photolibrary p. 12

Editor: Megan M. Gunderson
Art Direction & Cover Design: Neil Klinepier

Library of Congress Cataloging-in-Publication Data

Britton, Tamara L., 1963-
  Trapdoor spiders / Tamara L. Britton.
       p. cm. -- (Spiders)
  Includes index.
   ISBN 978-1-61613-443-3
  1. Trap-door spiders I. Title.
  QL458.4.B75 2011
  595.4'4--dc22
                              2010012785

CONTENTS

TRAPDOOR SPIDERS

Scientists recognize 109 spider families. Within these families, there are 38,000 species! About 114 species belong to the family **Ctenizidae**. These species are known as trapdoor spiders. They are found in North America.

There are unrelated members of other spider families that also build nests with doors. So they are called trapdoor spiders, too. These species live in parts of Asia, Argentina, and Africa. They can also be found in **temperate** areas of the Southern **Hemisphere**, such as Australia and New Zealand.

Whatever their family, all spiders are arachnids. They have two body parts and eight legs. All arachnids are arthropods. Their skeletons are on

Trapdoor spiders get their name from the homes they build. They dig burrows that are protected by a trapdoor!

the outside of their bodies. Spiders are also ectothermic. So, trapdoor spiders get their body temperature from their surroundings.

Sizes

For spiders, trapdoor spiders are fairly large. Many species reach a body length of more than 1 inch (2.5 cm). The female ravine trapdoor spider may measure 1.2 inches (3 cm). However, the male is only 0.75 inches (1.9 cm) long.

The California trapdoor spider is larger. It can reach 1.3 inches (3.3 cm) in length. The African red trapdoor spider is another large species. It can grow more than 1.6 inches (4 cm) long. Its leg span is about twice the length of its body!

Road and stream banks are favorite trapdoor spider building sites!

SHAPES

Like its relative the tarantula, the trapdoor spider has a robust body. A trapdoor spider has two body parts. These are the **cephalothorax** and the **abdomen**.

At the front of the cephalothorax is the spider's head. It holds two **pedipalps**. Between them are two **chelicerae**. The chelicerae are tipped with fangs!

Next, four pairs of short, stout legs line the sides of the cephalothorax. Claws at the end of each leg help the spider grip surfaces. Inside the cephalothorax are the spider's brain, **venom** glands, and stomach.

The spider's intestine, nerve cord, and blood vessels pass through the pedicel. This slim waist connects the cephalothorax with the abdomen.

Spider Anatomy

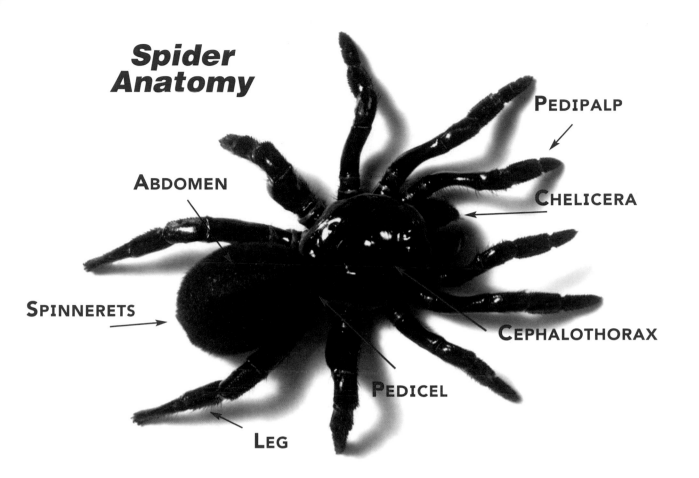

A trapdoor spider's **abdomen** contains its heart. It also holds its **digestive** tract, reproductive and respiratory **organs**, and silk glands. The silk glands make the spider's silk. The spider releases the silk from its body through its spinnerets.

COLORS

Trapdoor spiders have similar coloring. They range in color from brown to black. Their legs are darker than their bodies and are very shiny. In fact, the legs look like they have been polished!

The California trapdoor spider has common coloring. It has a brown or tannish **abdomen** and a dark brown **cephalothorax**. The legs and **chelicerae** are a darker brown.

The African red trapdoor spider has special coloring. It has a reddish shade to its legs, chelicerae, and cephalothorax. Its abdomen is tan, with a darker stripe lining the top.

African red trapdoor spiders live in southern Africa.

Where They Live

A trapdoor spider uses special teeth on its **chelicerae** to dig a tube-shaped burrow. The spider rolls the excavated dirt into a ball. It kicks the ball from the hole using **spines** on its back legs.

The deep burrow can reach more than 10 inches (25 cm) below ground! The burrow may be one tunnel. Or, several tunnels may branch out from the main tunnel. The spider lines the burrow with silk.

The trapdoor spider secures the burrow's opening with a door. The door is made from silk and mud.

A trapdoor spider may have more than one way to enter or exit its burrow.

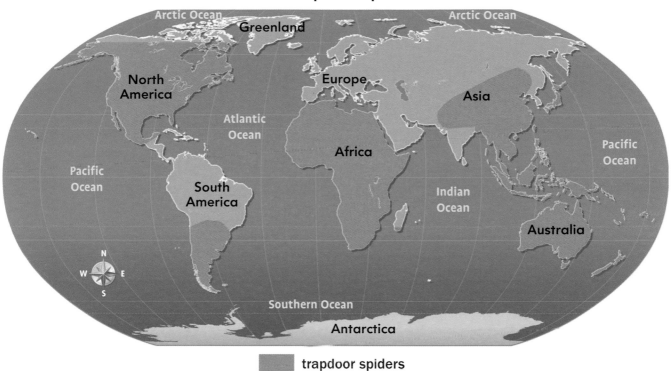

Where Do Trapdoor Spiders Live?

trapdoor spiders

Some doors are like corks. They plug the burrow like a stopper. Other doors are hinged, like the door to your room. Still others are split in the middle, like saloon doors in a cowboy movie!

The spider disguises its door with sticks and debris. This makes the burrow difficult to see. You could walk right by a trapdoor spider's home and not even know it!

SENSES

Trapdoor spiders have the same five senses as humans. Like most spiders, they have eight eyes. But their eyesight is not very sharp. Since they spend most of their time in burrows, good eyesight is not important.

Trapdoor spiders have special tubes on their legs and **pedipalps**. With these, the spiders can smell and taste.

The most important sense the trapdoor spider has is its ability to feel vibrations. The hairs on its legs and pedipalps sense the vibrations of animals passing by the burrow. This way, the spider knows exactly when a meal is within easy reach!

When grabbing prey, the trapdoor spider keeps its hind legs inside the burrow. That way, it can quickly retreat.

DEFENSE

The most important defense a trapdoor spider has is its burrow. It spends almost all of its time inside. If an enemy tries to open the trapdoor, the spider holds it closed with its **chelicerae**!

Some trapdoor spiders have extra defenses. For example, the ravine trapdoor spider has a hardened **abdomen**. When threatened, the spider heads for the bottom of its burrow. There, the abdomen makes a perfect plug. It gives the spider extra protection if the trapdoor fails to stop an invader.

The trapdoor spider must watch out for predatory wasps. A trapdoor is no match for these fierce creatures. They use their sharp jaws to chew their way right in!

Trapdoor spiders are timid and shy. But if they are threatened, they can bite! Luckily, their venom is not poisonous to humans.

FOOD

Trapdoor spiders eat all types of insects. These include beetles, ants, and grasshoppers. Lizards also make tasty treats.

As the spider sits in its burrow, it can feel the vibrations from nearby prey. When the prey passes the trapdoor, the spider leaps out and grabs it. The spider then drags its meal into the burrow.

The spider bites its prey and **injects** it with **venom**. Then, it pours **digestive** juices onto its prey. These liquefy the victim's body. Then, the spider sucks up its liquid meal.

Trapdoor spiders build their burrows in places where prey will likely walk by.

BABIES

To mate, a male trapdoor spider goes wandering in search of a female. He mates with the female in her burrow.

The female lays eggs in her burrow. She spins a silken egg sac around them. Then, she uses more silk and sticks the egg sac to the wall!

When the baby spiders hatch, they stay in the burrow with their mother. These spiderlings may live with her for as long as eight months. When it is time for them to leave, trapdoor spiderlings walk away. They do not **balloon**.

A young trapdoor spider then builds its own burrow. As it grows, it **sheds** its **exoskeleton**. This is called molting. It also builds a bigger burrow! Male trapdoor spiders do not live long after mating. Females can survive for 20 years!

As a trapdoor spider enlarges its burrow, it must make the door wider, too. These expansions can be seen on the door. They look like the growth rings on the inside of a tree trunk.

GLOSSARY

abdomen - the rear body section of an arthropod, such as an insect or a spider.

ballooning - using a strand of silk to catch the wind and move to a new location. This is a behavior of some spiders.

cephalothorax (seh-fuh-luh-THAWR-aks) - the front body section of an arachnid that includes the head and the thorax.

chelicera (kih-LIH-suh-ruh) - either of the front, leglike organs of an arachnid that has a fang attached to it.

Ctenizidae (tuh-NEYEZUH-dee) - the scientific name for the family of trapdoor spiders.

digestive - of or relating to the breakdown of food into simpler substances the body can absorb.

exoskeleton - the outer covering or structure that protects an animal, such as an insect.

hemisphere - one half of Earth.

inject - to force a fluid into the body, usually with a needle or something sharp.

organ - a part of an animal or a plant composed of several kinds of tissues. An organ performs a specific function. The heart, liver, gallbladder, and intestines are organs of an animal.

pedipalp (PEH-duh-palp) - either of the leglike organs of a spider that are used to sense motion and catch prey.

shed - to cast off hair, feathers, skin, or other coverings or parts by a natural process.

spine - a stiff, pointed projection on an animal.

temperate - having neither very hot nor very cold weather.

venom - a poison produced by some animals and insects. It usually enters a victim through a bite or a sting.

WEB SITES

To learn more about trapdoor spiders, visit ABDO Publishing Company on the World Wide Web at **www.abdopublishing.com**. Web sites about trapdoor spiders are featured on our Book Links page. These links are routinely monitored and updated to provide the most current information available.

INDEX